How to Hold a Fart in

The New Rules for Career Success

By
Don Henderson

Made in United States
North Haven, CT
15 July 2022

21377117R00182